# Leonard Cohen Is Dead

Also by Carolyn Cordon and published by Ginninderra Press
*Tense and Still*

Carolyn Cordon

# Leonard Cohen Is Dead
## People poems

*Leonard Cohen Is Dead: People poems*
ISBN 978 1 76109 321 0
Copyright © text Carolyn Cordon 2022
Cover image from Pixabay

First published 2022 by
**GINNINDERRA PRESS**
PO Box 3461 Port Adelaide 5015
www.ginninderrapress.com.au

# Contents

| | |
|---|---|
| Introduction | 9 |
| Leonard Cohen is dead | 11 |
| May peace reign | 13 |
| The Constant Deafening of Life | 14 |
| Lunchtime Realisation | 15 |
| 65 King William Street early 80s | 16 |
| My Inside/Outside Life | 18 |
| Mindfully Community-minded | 20 |
| Two Plus One Equals Three | 21 |
| Ages, stages | 23 |
| Blue sky above | 24 |
| Life Lesson | 25 |
| A Place Called Home | 26 |
| We are trees | 27 |
| It's raining in the desert | 28 |
| My Because Poem | 29 |
| Life is for Living | 30 |
| Saving Lives | 31 |
| Hot water | 33 |
| On Feeling Cold | 35 |
| Many Forms | 36 |
| Precious Sista | 37 |
| Pathology | 38 |
| Night Sky | 39 |
| My White Genes | 40 |
| Everyone's Business | 41 |
| Some things are unforgivable | 42 |
| Smart Lady | 44 |
| Unless | 45 |

| | |
|---|---:|
| When the time is right | 46 |
| Me Too – Some Ideas | 47 |
| Testing Times | 48 |
| Thoughts on Friendship | 51 |
| Welcome to our Word World! | 52 |
| Language is a tool | 53 |
| The Truth About Life | 54 |
| Death Lurks | 56 |
| Writing Advice For Ducks | 57 |
| Pauline Hanson's Bumslide Downward | 58 |
| Beware the Hungry Owl | 59 |
| Thoughts About Birds & Trees | 60 |
| Another Day at Home | 62 |
| A Call to Action | 63 |
| A step too far | 65 |
| Hospital Waiting | 66 |
| On the Road to a Resolution | 67 |
| Happy He's Home | 68 |
| Lived Experience | 69 |
| On Having Enough | 71 |
| Feeling settled, but leaving soon | 72 |
| Flying Observations | 74 |
| Free Speech? | 76 |
| When Life is Good | 77 |
| Falling | 78 |
| Who Was David Niven Anyway? | 79 |
| My Preferred Ways | 80 |
| Baby blue | 81 |
| The Big C | 82 |
| The Skin We're In | 83 |
| Rusty Thoughts | 84 |
| Finding My Starring Role | 85 |

| | |
|---|---:|
| Leaving a Mark | 87 |
| No forgetting some things? | 88 |
| After Bushfires | 89 |
| Watching | 90 |
| It's Just Not Cricket! | 91 |
| Go Team! | 92 |
| An End of Year Lament | 93 |
| Deeper Lives | 94 |
| Lest We Forget | 96 |

# Introduction

We're born, we live and then we die. And along the way, we may fall in love, or lust, make love, fight, kiss and make up, if we're lucky. And we find people – collaborators, friends, those lovers I mentioned, in passing. If we are writers, we reach out to people, at times, to talk with, go places with. And sometimes we spy on people... It isn't a nasty thing, this spying, it's just what we have to do, to know more about what people are, or can be. If we watch enough, and learn enough, we will better understand who and what people are. Poets will write small snippets, perhaps a eulogy, or an elegy... And of course poets will write their own life out in lines, and verses, hiding their own truth in the clouds, or the trees, nature, or the sky, they write poems about, and the life they write about becomes many things, some brutally true, some encased in hints and fibs, hiding the truth, while exposing it in different ways.

I don't claim there is a literal truth in every poem in this collection, although the title of this work, and the first poem of the same name, they are true. Leonard Cohen is indeed dead. The other poems in the collection? Ah, that would be telling! But true or not, I hope you find them at least interesting, and some of them even intriguing, who knows?

I have written some of the poems here in response to writing prompts, or to five-word challenges at the Adelaide Plains Poets Chapter and Verse Writing group, or at the Gawler Poets at the Pub event, or perhaps in response to challenges on the *Words Out Loud* radio program with Joanne Baker on PBA PM 89.7, which I have been involved in, before Covid came along and changed things...

So thanks, Alex and Joanne, for those writing prompts you've given us, making us groan at times but rise to the challenge with our written responses, in beautiful ways, over and over again. Alex Robertson, in particular, I thank you for your part in the making of this collection.

Tricking our minds to find inspirational poetry and prose, with the lamest of prompts, what an amazing thing it is!

I hope you will find this poetry collection to be an amazing thing too, and I wish you well in your reading of my words!

Carolyn Cordon

# Leonard Cohen is dead

Leonard Cohen is dead, never again
will he perform his own songs, live
with that voice loaded up, with him,
his ideas, his words, his being, him…

Yes Leonard Cohen has died, but,
but, but, surely we need him here
with us, as we try to construct anew
ways to do and say and fucking be.

We let him go, hidden inside a movie
a kids' movie for God's Sake! Him!
With his voice of gravel, smoothed
with silken tones and made afresh

every single time we see that video
of him in concert, giving his all,
so we learn how to give our all –
to love, to life, to all that matters.

Leonard Cohen has died, but
but, oh but…I so wish he was here
still alive, still doing his thing, over
and over, his voice, his words, him…

Leonard has died, but will live on
for as long as we all remember
how much we loved him, and he
loved us, singing his heart out,

giving himself. So he may be dead,
but we all hold a piece of him alive,
somewhere, in our head, or heart,
or gut, somewhere inside, and true.

## May peace reign

Jumbled violence,
accusations hurled,
understanding
non-existent.
Friendly discussion
becomes interesting
conversation, and then
friendly banter,
as speakers begin
to appreciate words shared.
In this way the world
may finally become
what it should always
have been.

# The Constant Deafening of Life

Modern life, the screeching, scraping, soul-destroying sound of it. Yelling, shouting, blasting, bellowing, the noise, the noise, the noise of it, why won't they just shut up?
Oh for the sounds of a bird, native to the forest we want to be in, calling to others, for reasons we don't understand, perhaps, but still beautiful to hear... Calling to others – looking for a mate, warning of danger? Loud, perhaps, but loud for a reason, not just for the sake of sound.

Sound, more, and more sound... If only clashing extraneous noise was gone, the truth of all may be heard, but for the Bang! Crash! racket of life, drowning out the quiet truth of what is important, drowning it out, as strident advertising suffocates us, and we're trapped, tense, terrified, unable to hear the quiet sound of a bird flying past, the swoosh of breezes in trees, buzzing bees in blossom, soft whimpers of a puppy needing a feed, or a child needing a hug. Or the sound of the one you love, gently saying, 'I love you', as you stand together, in the quiet of a forest, with no harsh mechanical sound around. Silence, lovely silence, but for natural sounds...

I wonder, would I hear better now, if I could have lived my life quietly, rather than suffering, through life circumstances, the near-constant damaging and deafening cacophony of modern life?
    Oh, for the blissful peace of the sweet sound of silence...

# Lunchtime Realisation

At my husband's former work's Christmas lunch –
I look around, see faces I used to know, in a
different life, from a very long time ago…
I used to work there too, before… Before

I became mother, artsy community person –
writing creatively, helping others do the same,
something I'd never have done if I'd stayed,
at the office, where these people gave their lives.

These worthy, professional, uni-educated ones,
whose role was to think law and such matters,
while I, fresh out of high school, public-educated,
my role of minion was to fetch, file and deliver –

copy machine my main tool, while for these people,
the brain was theirs… I know these people, they
know me, but the divide, the cultural split between us,
still holds, even at this Christmas lunch, where

I look around & know, deep within my marrow,
these people, though worthy, are not my people,
and never will be. Our needs are the same, but
thoughts, wants & values are profoundly different.

# 65 King William Street early 80s

A home to many, a haven
for those who craved
a place to rest for a couple
of years, then move on.

Or one where talents
in thinking, & drinking
merged, & at end of week,
knock off, head for tavern,

get a drink, sit down, chat.
Get another, stay awhile,
going over week's doings,
then catch a bus home…

The ATO, clerks with eyes
on power, clerical assistants
with eyes on the weekend,
ambitionless ones, unless

they stuck there long enough,
learnt the ropes, moving
through the ranks, ever upward
or just stayed, powerless…

Fond memories, of 18 floors
of friendship, drama, but also
boredom too, filing, delivering,
down stairs or up them, constant.

It's changed now, the Tax Office,
split up, moved, some of us gone,
retired, but still get together
once a year, to relive it all…

Glory days, or not, the ATO
still lives large in memories
of those of us who gave it
our best, or a close proximity!

Carrying folder, or paper & pen
stood in for 'working', & hid any
shirking – things got done or didn't,
& as long as reports were reported

to government, proof of actions
undertaken, results attained or
reasons for it given, if not. Five
days a week, lifts going up &

down, up & down, with very few
ever giving a look at that glorious view
from the top. But I saw it once, us
lowly ones stuck together & shared.

## My Inside/Outside Life

Sitting inside, looking out,
I see cars passing by,
& trees with waving branches –
waving hello to me? No, just
waving, as the dictates
of the breeze insisted…

Inside with me, are Missy,
& the TV screen.
Missy & I both ignore
screen's action. Superbowl?
Pfft, who cares? Not us,
none of our business.

What is our business?
Is it inside or outside?
Missy is pet dog,
self-installed 'guard' dog,
hubby's walking companion,
so for her it's both.

My business is, hmm, what?
Writing? Community stuff?
'Business' is a textured word,
spiky with taxation obligations
& other rules & regulations,
but can be rewarding, too…

I'm a pensioner, my 'business'
untainted by money, & taxation,
unless my business was to
take off, with increased sales
of my books, climbing above &
beyond inside/outside constraints.

I'm still waiting on that one. But
for now, writing & community, writing
about community, just writing – poems,
a novel, articles, writing my way into
things, bigger & better, than my usual
inside/outside life, this is enough…

## Mindfully Community-minded

We're at the oval, & the new group
Is like that oval, fresh but green,
Sometimes worn down by the traffic
Of life's passing, pounding footsteps
Grinding down possible growth,
But with the knowledge that a good rain
At the right time, can refresh us, & with
A glowing goodness, rejuvenate us…

This town's oval is a space for all, a
Gathering place, with friends, or soon
To be friends, sharing stories, ideas,
Moments. Breathing in happiness
And breathing out things harmful,
Hurtful. We're making room for more –
More moments to think on, consider,
Finding strength in mindful moments.

## Two Plus One Equals Three

Greed or need, what's mine is yours
and vice versa, including chores?
No, that won't work, I can't manage
vacuuming – too tiring, causes damage.

Solved with quiet negotiation,
no hateful words, or angry frustration.
Living together, two peaceful doves,
no nasty slurs, no painful shoves…

Raising our child, my happiest work,
those duties, ones I'd never shirk.
But he's grown-up now, our only son
but visits regularly for food and fun.

Jake's our boy, but he's also his own,
his qualities shine brighter as he's grown.
He brings his parents so much joy,
our wise and caring, handsome boy!

This Valentine's Day just gone past
zipped right by us both, super fast –
no need to loudly profess our bond,
love a precious, refreshing frond…

Thirty-four years of married life
plus two years before 'husband and wife',
retired now, lives winding down?
No, both busy, volunteers in town.
Our country lives, with the community
add much to overarching humanity –
helping out becomes a normal mode,
travelling along our connected road.

## Ages, stages

Births, deaths, marriages…
Happy, sad and joyful –
moments in life's crazy jigsaw;
you get the hand life deals you,
it's your task to play the cards well.

Poker, patience, gin rummy,
whatever the game, do your best –
winners are grinners, losers shrug
awaiting the next game, or fold,
going home, can be the best idea…

Feeling sad, but with good news too,
yes, life is a jumbled mix of stuff,
& who can say they've had enough
when none can know how much they
can take, until the game of life is done.

# Blue sky above

A vision of blue through windowpane,
white-tipped waves slide in/out, so close…
No shark around to bring on fear, just
wave, after wave, of rippling sea, again,
again, with seagull-provided soundtrack.

When I look up at my own blue sky,
the plains reach out to my heart – I know
the horizon surrounds me, embracing…
The sea a welcome distraction, I'll visit
gladly for friendship, but then head home.

# Life Lesson

A long table of 'community elders',
they chat, share tips and memories
as I watch and listen, alone but for
coffee and cake, at my own table.
They're mostly women, but some
men too, the hair of them all, various
shades of grey except for a few,
hiding from age? Their dark hair
luxurious with life, but their voices
seem lessened, dimmed, and I
wonder, does grey hair impart
wisdom, that hair dye washes out,
or is it something I'll have to wait
to find out, until I'm a more venerable
age? A life lesson to come, in time?

# A Place Called Home

This place, country, but manageable
with room for what we want,
and a bit more, we're happy to share
it all, with birds, insects, even
reptiles, if they don't bother us.

Been here over 30 years, brought up dogs,
then our own child, joined groups,
attended events, then began
to organise some things ourselves.
Suburbanites turned country folk.

Giving back to those who've given
so much to us. Finding our way
into what suits us best, learning
to love, or at least endure, the dust,
even finding pride in a dirty car!

And the trees, the splendour
of the night sky, delight of blue skies,
those horizons that stretch as far
as far can go, lovely! And rainbows,
rain on a tin roof, galahs to smile at.

Yes, my son is country-born and bred,
and in my very bones, I realise the truth,
while the suburbs trained my ways,
educated me, and the city gave me work,
I am country now, it's where I belong!

## We are trees

Stand up tall, upper limbs stretched, reaching
for the sun, the rain, the rest of your forest,
lower limbs reaching down, as gravity dictates,
downward as your roots find connections.
Twist your roots around theirs, grow together
or apart, as seems right… You keep on thinking,
thinking, about how blinking shuts out, lets in,
shuts out, the light, and remember that time when,
eyes shut tight against your best ever thing,
you missed it, missed out, or lost it, and on losing it,
choose a different thing instead, a better thing,
and you realised, eventually, eventually, it was never
things you needed, anyway, you just wanted them –
you wanted things, but needed connections…
Understand that – it's connections you need, always,
not things – connections to self, your own self,
and those other selves, those who get it – how you
see shapes in the clouds, and feel lonely in crowds,
because they see shapes too, and feel the loneliness
crowds can bring. While all of us – cloud lovers,
crowd haters, seek other kinds of crowds, crowds
of green, forests – where trees connect underground,
roots entwined, to seek out trees that give us all life,
instead of stark, soulless, breath-sucking crowds
of couldn't-care-less humanity, then, only then,
can we see the truths about humans, and trees,
and connections. Without roots, and connections
to take up nourishment, we will die, frail, dried out,
rootless, alone, alone, alone, and lonely.

# It's raining in the desert

after tropical ex-cyclone Esther

Yes, Esther, she's an ex now,
but she has plenty to spill –
better watch out, you've been warned,
it won't be safe until
she's wrenched out, dried out,
drained, nothing left inside.
Esther's glory days are over,
but she hasn't run away to hide –
once the eye of the storm,
she's got trouble still to cause
not so deadly, but not over yet.
At a river crossing? Pause –
look both ways, consider,
can you really make it through?
Because it's raining in the desert,
and Esther has news for you.

# My Because Poem

Because we live, we will die
Because we love, we may sigh
Because we grieve, we will cry
Because we think, we question why.

# Life is for Living

Driving home, as carefully as I can,
but after a drop or two, or more
careful is only a myth… Eyes
droop ever downward, attention
gone, eyes closed, asleep, then…

Oh shit! Wake up! Wake up!
Pull over, heart pounding, eyes
wide open, I'm awake, alive!
Last few minutes, driving home –
almost my life's final moments…

It happened too many times, long
straight road, then the bend, nearly
home, pressure off. Nearly dead…
Restart engine, indicate, drive off,
turn, and finally, home, safe at last.

Lesson learnt, make a vow –
Home is where I drink, not out,
or only with a driver. Staying alive,
if you drive, means drink comes
second, so living always wins!

## Saving Lives

Gluttony would never be my sin
My needs for food are scant
Quality preferred over quantity
The little that lasts for long

I value my health, look after self,
Vegetables and fruit my friends
Carrots over banana's delights
Savoury over sweet…

Food's not a vice to bring me down
I dine with decorous nibbles
No shoving food down in hasty gulps
That's not the way I go in life.

Looking at vices, sloth, that's mine
Not proud of that, but there's worse…
Sitting and thinking, I call it, but
Is that really the truth? I think it is.

I'm a poet, words will light my fuse
Line produced after thoughtful line.
Does anyone else know or care?
Can my words save people's lives?

Actually, yes, I think they can –
I've connected to others at times
Poetry written at a slothful rate
Or lines scribbled out in haste –

Connection can help healing come,
Knowing you're not alone
Not weird, unwanted, any more,
When another understands.

## Hot water

I get edgy
At the edges
And stay there
Waiting
To see a glimpse
Of what it is
That's coming next

But glimpses aren't
The whole truth
And are open
To misinterpretation
To misunderstanding
To missed steps
On life's road

I know this,
I show this
My wisdom etched
In my bones
On my lumpy
And bumpy skin
In my eyes

The next thing
Doesn't wait,
It happens
Ready or not –
Wisdom knows
Waiting to see
May sometimes fail

But jumping right in
Without hesitation
No second thoughts
No further
Consideration
Could land me
In hot water.

## On Feeling Cold

Knowing that the cold
is only moments away
from finding warmth –
living my 'flick of switch
put on a jumper'
life of relative ease

heat and cold easily
managed, well away
from lives suffered by
homeless people,
who have a no switch
to flick, & no jumper.

## Many Forms

Half envious of others,
but burdened with
memories
of life's swings
& roundabouts,
knowing being lonely
can hurt but
knowing too,
being alone
can be freedom
from many
forms of pain....

# Precious Sista

You passed the test, you are the best
now don't you blow it sista!
Don't trash your art cos you lost your heart
to some dumb-arse pisshead mister.

It's in your soul, it makes you whole
no need for pricks like that.
His attitude, if I may be rude
is that of a mindless prat!

You put your heart into your art
he laughs at it and mocks –
if he really knew, and loved you true
not just cos you wash his jocks,

if he understood, and treated you good
then he might just be the one…
But men who hold their woman like gold
are rare – blokes like their fun.

And fun to men, well sometimes, then –
a woman, she is hurtin';
drunken jokes, and loveless pokes
they'll happen, that's for certain.

But if you have a man, not an also-ran,
who takes your test and passes,
then don't be meek, he's one to keep
not those other deadbeat arses!

# Pathology

not my story, but true for others...

His pathological hatred,
my frozen love, iced over
by the way he loved, then
hated people l call friends.
Discombobulation rules me.
His face, a mask, one he can
put on and take off at will.
I ignored the tiny voice
inside my head, my heart,
that whispers, 'Go, go now!'
I stay, another woman
mistakenly thinking I can
perform a miracle, turn
a needy and vile man into
a lamb of a person. Wolf
to lamb? It can't happen,
my bruises prove it.
I know that now, I listen
to myself, remembering
to be ready, when it's right
to go, and to go, next time.

# Night Sky

Moon and Venus are there
amongst the stars
all shining down on us
as we squabble and scrape
through the dirt.
Every now and then,
why not leave hate behind?
Look up and wonder
at the gracious harmony
of night sky's beauty –
travel there in your dreams
of what life could be…
what you could become…
Move closer to the harmony
of that lovely night-time lesson
and aim your thoughts higher
and make your wishes broader.
Embrace the beauty and hope
as the vista above shines down
and shows how life could be.

## My White Genes

When my ancestors arrived
were people there waiting,
ready to welcome them
from one land to another?

Cornwall to South Australia –
a long journey in a big boat
hoping beyond hope
to find a brand-new home.

But what of those who already
called that river their home,
already living in and around
my ancestors' promised land?

Were the two sides friendly?
Did negotiations proceed
in a courteous manner?
Or is there ancestral guilt

holding on from that past,
and if so, how to assuage
that guilt, make penance,
apologise? I say I'm sorry,

the guilt though, remains.
Who knows from whom
I should ask forgiveness,
my white genes ask.

## Everyone's Business

He had a highwayman's
uncanny talent of
confounding her,
making a train wreck
of her crumbling confidence,
and leaving her thinking
she was at fault, again…
And with both he, and she
blaming her, not him,
she 'sucked it up, princess',
like he told her to, feeling
not a thing, like a princess…
The truth of it confounded
her friends too, but they
never said anything
because, he always seemed
like a nice bloke, you know?
And even if what she said
was true, doing anything
about it, well that would be
interfering, wouldn't it?
And it wasn't really any
of their business, was it?

## Some things are unforgivable

Where there is no redemptive will,
there can be no true forgiveness.
Without forgiving yourself,
there can be no inner peace.

We all are human, frail, flawed.
Some think though, about life,
choices, chances, demands,
benefits, costs. Studying results

regarding when, and what if,
or whether, x or y or even z
happened, or might, could or
would have happened, if…

If what? Yes – a wise question
to think on, if what? Was it
a fine day, or foul? Was there
no one present or a crowd?

But if you were there, you know,
and if you know, and did nothing,
what could you done? Nothing?
Or something? Without even

thinking on such things, how
can you affirm, no blame lies
with you, when there are a million
un- or ill-considered actions

and truths… Go back, look,
think, consider, surmise, revise.
Decide to apologise. Forgiveness
sought, and given, good for all?

## Smart Lady

Love seemed abundant,
the dream so real –
emotions aplenty,
he seemed 'A good deal'.

He began playing games,
she grew less fond,
got out quick,
and got the bond.

# Unless

If I do this, it will be great
I can hold my head up high,
unless…

Unless I do it and it's crap
so crawl away, and want to die,
& unless…

Someone else gets there first
cos they run much faster than I
& unless

It turns out I did the wrongest thing
when I ran instead of fly
& unless

Being loud & proud is wrong,
you should be meek and shy
& unless –

Unless rules are there to show us
women are weak and they all cry
but unless

we all believe them when they
tell that dirty rotten lie
then truth will come out kicking.

Truth will set us free
and all of us can rise up higher than the sky
unless,

Yes, unless…

# When the time is right

Time is a burden, a guard, restriction. It's having to
do this, now. It's not being allowed to do that, ever.
It's only being allowed to do it when they say you can…
Working for 'the man', not yourself, living within
society's rules, family rules, your religion's rules…

But time is also a promise, a commitment, an opportunity
too. When schooling is over, you can do so much more.
When you're tall enough, you'll be able to reach high.
When you're an adult, you can be whatever it is you want
to be, you can do it all! Child to teen, to adult, to aged…

Time measured by calendars, watches, by sun, & stars,
& moon. Measured by Nature – growing seasons come,
and go, plants will flower, fruit will grow, but only when
the time is right, & if sunshine & water are there too.
Nature's time is true time, our time unneeded, sometimes…

Mankind's greatest challenge – in this tyranny of needing it
now & with not enough time, isn't to acquire more, to go
to war, to dig up things, & make killing machines. Humanity's
greatest challenge is to find the time, the right time, to think
& consider things wisely, and then act, not thoughtlessly react.

The fast thing is the disaster thing…the crying thing,
the dying thing, a time when apologies go unsaid, innocence
& care are dead, our bodies stuffed, but our brains unfed…
We look to the future, wonder when the time will be right, but
the time to do what is right is not in the future, it's right NOW!

## Me Too – Some Ideas

When I was young and felt his tongue
Pushing down my throat
I didn't like it, not at all
That horrid randy old goat

The 'he' here covers many men
From family to friends and more
Born a girl, it goes with the turf
But I didn't know what was in store…

I don't know names of all the men
Who've invaded my personal space
I've tried to forget the details too
To disappear without a trace…

But then I saw Me Too arrive
Realised anger's an emotion too
I've decided to ditch the word ashamed
And hope my sistas can too

We didn't ask to be assaulted,
Felt up, abused or raped
Having tits and a vagina though
That's how our life journey's shaped

# Testing Times

After the laughter
After the tears
The lies that came true
The unreasonable fears

Then came the hugs
And understanding
Scarred, not scared
And less demanding

Those who expect
While never giving
Just take, take, take
From the barely living

Givers though,
are always there
Build others up
No hateful privileged stare

They wipe tears away
Quash every myth
Do good for all
Both kin and kith

Showing the truth
In every lie
Honest, always
Until they die…

If you know one
Of this worthy crew
If you've seen yourself
The good they do

Why not stay
Keep on watching
See them finesse
What others are botching

And after watching
Why not join in
Do good yourself
And all can win

Give to others
Help the needy
Show better ways
To the greedy

We all have inside
Waiting to evolve
A need to help
To problem-solve

Societies are made
Of ordinary people
Living lives 'Now'
Not as a sequel

The best of them
Show not tell
Calmly doing
No need to yell

They get on and do
Not lay blame
Realise this truth
And try the same

Not all can do
Their very best
But give it a go?
You pass the test!

## Thoughts on Friendship

A heedless word spoken in jest
Not understanding, too demanding
Boundaries rise up high

You don't realise, you failed the test
Middle-class privilege, talking garbage
Others weep and sigh

One day may come, deeper thought
Mind distracted, words retracted,
They both hug and cry

Friendship, to one who feels distraught
If you muck it up, you suck it up
Mindful till you die

Women are made of many a stripe –
Deep thinking, or heavy drinking
(nearly as much as a guy)

Wise words from some, others talk tripe
It's up to you, to think it through
Which is truth, which lie?

To have good friends, don't be a dunce –
Don't measure them, treasure them
Lest friendless days loom nigh

The friends you may have wanted once
All a con, thankfully gone
To have good ones, care and try.

# Welcome to our Word World!

Pondering, wondering,
Not pandering or wandering.
Such confusing things, vowels…
I salute all who conquer English
as their second language –
Well done to you all!

# Language is a tool

For building up, breaking down
For romancing, enhancing
Verbs are doing words – nail
meanings in tight, etch away
lies to find meaning. Nouns
are things, wedding rings,
broken vows and plates,
flowers, missiles – things,
things, more bloody things…

We speak, misspeak, lie,
contrive. Language a tool
we use for ourselves, against
ourselves. Our self-hatred
ripping flesh from our body,
bleeding, in pain, bandaged
up with lies, calming untruths
and half-truths, forgetting
actual truth ever was…

Unless we can break free,
and remind ourselves, again
that the truth is out there
if we're brave enough to look
and then tell what we see…
Open our hearts, souls,
and minds to it, glory in it.
Reach for it, teach it, earn it,
learn it, know it, and show it.

# The Truth About Life

based on a Facebook post, some years back

What's life all about?
Good question,
this one…
yeah life –
you want the truth?
You gotta live it,
throw up on it,
remember it,
forget it,
angst over it,
forgive yourself for it,
forgive those others.
Who? You know who…

Think about it all again
then based on your thoughts
unforgive them,
remember stuff
forget it again
then forgive yourself
once,
twice,
thrice times more…
realise you've moved
beyond –

below
above
and well away
from what others label as life
but what feels like
prison to you –
and you're still not
even close yet,
to finally knowing
what life is all about.

## Death Lurks

The world is a circus
where monkeys, lions, clowns
& whip-cracking ringmasters
encourage desperate acts
from those whose work
depends on convincing
audiences the possibility
of death in various forms
lurks nearby, waiting…
That's Entertainment.

# Writing Advice For Ducks

'Daffy like the duck
is great if you are stuck –
creative maybe, but looks like muck.
You're maybe thinking, at writing you suck,
keep on going, get ideas out, like a chook's egg, & cluck!
Writing, when good, takes brain work, more than it takes luck.
Do your best, accept both praise and blame, don't pass the buck…
Better stop, lest I write something rude,
& ensure no profanity will intrude!'

# Pauline Hanson's Bumslide Downward

The iconic mountainous
height – to climb or not
to climb? Those here
before us whitefellas,
say no, and whether
they're asking or telling us
not to, isn't really
the point, is it? Because
when the name changed,
from Ayers Rock, to Uluru,
surely that rock became
unclimbable, didn't it?

# Beware the Hungry Owl

a poem in 'near rhyme'

Wise owl
night watching –
a silly fool,
head scratching –
man's purpose unclear…
Owl's steady stare;
wise bird waits,
with no complaints –
Silly itching duff,
he's ripping off
his cerebrals!

No surprises –
Owl, claw-reaches,
its hunger aroused;
man retches.
Brain bits to scoop –
a bloodied soup,
man falls down,
owl follows to dine.
'Love fresh brains,'
owl claims,
'yummy for my meals!'

# Thoughts About Birds & Trees

Branch-arms outstretched reach up
to the sun, and out, to my heart. Not
my beloved Eucalyptus trees this time,
but trees with a different, not personal
history. Aleppo Pine, Lone Pine, given
to farmers in the region, to do, what?
Remember the war? Commemorate those
who fell, and never returned? I leave
that history for others – not my war, not
my story. Other wars touch me more –
squabbling birds, sexy birds, male birds
showing off to the ladies, who choose,
or are taken, in various birdish ways.
Seduce, copulate, make nest, egg lay,
sit on, then hatch! Strong secure branches
embrace nests, wind blows branches,
rocking nest with growing chicks, whose
feathers come in, and short practice
flights commence, as windblown fluff
drifts from tree height to ground, awaiting
next nesting season? I watch, my human
thoughts bird-brained? Some of them,
sure, but I do so like watching, thinking,
dreaming, learning, as the birds go about
their birdly days, and the pine trees stand,
proud and tall. Rough bark, strong, straight
trunks, pine cones, and poking needles,

that fall, creating a soft landing ground
below. Protection for those chicks, in case
of falls? Or coincidence? Nature's grand
schemes, tests… Life grows, survives,
and thrives or doesn't, and so doesn't
move forward. But even in death they
give life to others. Nature 'heartless',
but honest, with a deeper kind of care.
Humans, full of heart, but in reality, liars,
cheats, and so more truly heartless.

## Another Day at Home

not my true story, but there by the grace of whatever

Tethered to the task, the shot of steam
brings some excitement to her tedious job,
the smoothing, then hanging of clothes,
her partner's work clothes – white shirts,
dark trousers, pair after relentless pair.

Their toddler on the floor is suddenly
not on the floor, nowhere in sight, where
is she, where is she? Their dog barks,
Woof, woof, then runs into the room,
wet feet marking the slate tiles.

Wet feet? 'Maddy, what are you up to, Maddy?'
she calls, but in her head she sees
the nappy bucket, only partly filled,
but is it enough to drown a child? Maddy
silent as death, crawls into the room

dripping nappy over her head, smiling
at funny Mummy, who scoops her up, whizzes
her around and follows water trail to now
flooded bathroom. Sighing, she runs the bath
again, strips off and climbs in with her child.

# A Call to Action

Dreary, dry, & devilish dust
Gets in eyes & clothes & home
Cleaning it out, we really must,
So out comes toxic cleaning foam…

But wait, what substance is this?
Down from dark clouds in a rush
Is Mother Nature taking a piss?
Whatever, it is, it comes in a gush!

Is it Mother Nature's idea of a joke?
Climate changes, a merry dance,
blame being laid, fingers point and poke
many locked in a denialist trance.

'Not my fault, you're to blame!'
Denials come from those in charge,
government heedless, shows no shame,
while problems loom ever large.

From dust, to rain, from dry to wet,
from day to day, ever onward –
Is this is good as it's going to get
travelling rapidly back, not forward?

While some rise up, taking action
plants and animals all suffer still.
Can better ideas ever take traction?
Things get better? Do I think they will?

Do I think that? No, merely hope,
from hope to action, a mighty leap.
Climate change isn't just a trope,
ignored by people who act like sheep –

They read the paper, believe the words
buy the products advertised –
an ignorant bloody flock of turds,
there's deaths, haven't they realised?

Animals, plants, habitats, people –
First fire, now flood, the changes hit.
Me & you, and all of those sheeple
look around, rise up, & do your bit!

## A step too far

Oh, such a fuss!
Pain ensued, baring
of simple truths –
Bones when broken,
are rarely helpful
in enhancing calm,
but are excellent
at teaching you
what you can
endure.

## Hospital Waiting

Waiting for ambulance to arrive,
Waiting for the ambos' decision on
If to go to hospital & where to go.
Waiting to head off, to get there,
To be admitted, to see this expert,
Or that. Waiting for tests, meds.
Waiting for diagnoses, for meals,
For procedures, for more tests,
More results. Waiting to get better
Waiting to understand why
Still waiting on that one, always –
Why? Waiting, waiting, and waiting…
Why? Just because.

# On the Road to a Resolution

The way is winding, like the bandages
formerly wound around my lower leg,
holding together the good works done.

Bandages all gone, medical procedures
completed, now recovery is my task
not someone else's now. Can I do it?

So far, yes, actually, I'm exercising
daily – physio and others, as diligently
as those former procedures performed.

Early days yet, these things, bones
healing, body and mind confidence
merging, slowly, but surely, I hope…

Are balance and strength increasing?
I hope so, yes – falling over isn't on my
New Year's Eve list of things to do!

# Happy He's Home

Was I happy he was coming home again?
Of course I was, he's my greatest friend.
Happily married for a million years,
But why, oh why these blasted tears?
I know, of course I've been feeling stressed,
I know I should've been feeling blessed.
But I wasn't being treated like a blessed being,
Copping critiques, why wasn't he seeing,
He's not the only one been doing it tough,
And his passenger seat driving was way too much!
Once home looking like the place was a mess,
Well, I'm not a cleaner, mate, I'm a fucking princess!

## Lived Experience

You've lived together
For so many years
You almost know
The hairs in his ears

As he now knows
Each of your socks
& you're well acquainted
With his jocks…

Fully naked
Fully dressed
You're comfortable
With both, not stressed

And when it's time
For a little 'action'
Our lumps or bumps
Meet favourable reaction

Familiarity brings,
Not contempt, but
Greater love, any gates
Between, open not shut

Living, breathing
Loving, knowing
Giving respect
That's always showing

The number of years
Makes me proud
We've done this
Together, shout out loud!

Good and bad,
The times all flow
You knuckle down
And make it so

Seeing others fail
At this marriage game
Is sad, I've won & wish
They had the same

But getting lucky
In matrimony
Takes so much more
Than just a ceremony.

# On Having Enough

Happy or sad, is it by choice?
Tears or laughter, weep or rejoice?
Is it up to us all, how we react?

When life seems good, why is it so?
Accept it you think, or let it go?
Some say their life's already jam-packed,

No time for fun, business to do
Others say, 'Grab it and you can have some too!'
I say it all can be good, and that's a fact!

It's how you see it, that's the thing…
Does it make you smile, cause your heart to sing?
Then take it up gently, show some tact

Treasure the good fortune, never gloat
Your favoured thing may not rock every boat.
There's plenty in life, our planet is stacked

With sunshine and trees, glorious stuff
Just take what you need, that's enough.
When people get greedy, the contract is cracked

Taking without giving, stealing from others
Paying no heed to their sisters and brothers
Empathy is what those people lacked…

I have enough now, and hope you do too
If not, here's a little, I'll share some with you –
Live your own life, near enough, if not exact

# Feeling settled, but leaving soon

I'm parked, on the main street
Two Wells, South Australia,
Friday afternoon, the time is
coming up to 2 p.m., and life
is looking good. Sitting here,
cars drive past, both ways…
people walking from shop
to shop, to car, or home, once
the shopping is all done…

I can see other living things
too, smaller creatures, on,
next to, and flying above,
the road. Birds, and insects
of course. There are always
insects. Because of where
and when this is – summer,
Adelaide Plains, there are bound
to be snakes, somewhere…

There's a breeze, gentle, calm,
I watch branches of the trees
and bushes sway, palm tree
fronds sway too, and from inside
of my car the sky seems to be
an unsullied sweep of pure blue.
But our dog, Missy, is home,
waiting for me, to feed her,
let her out and then back in.

So, soon, yes, soon, easy
does it, time to get going,
Two Wells duties done, time
to go. Turn key to start the car,
check rear vision mirror – clear,
no traffic. Pull out, head home,
where Missy's tail will wag
and she'll gratefully tuck into
her lunch, as I will with mine.

# Flying Observations

Wings, flight –
fly high,
swoop low,
ride hot thermals,
drift, squawk –
birds speak,
we hear,
but don't know
what they say.
Wise words?
Who can know?
We live our lives
birds and humans
separate…
But cars & birds,
crash deaths –
bird lives lost,
connecting
through grief…
I mourn them
these victims
every one.
Metal monsters
kill with no regrets,
while drivers
drive on,
busy, heedless
or aware
and mourning
as I mourn too,

on seeing
remnants
of the battle –
scattered feathers,
& limp body, never
to rise again
into the air.
Yes, every one
a tragedy.

# Free Speech?

A sonnet

Their words inspire bad ways, not good,
I wish to clench my ears to keep them out –
they sicken me, why listen? I know I should
cleanse my skin of them, scream and shout…
Though my pores refuse to let them in,
still hate invades my conflicted self.
To listen, to hear their filth, is it sin?
I'm complicit – ghoul, not goodly elf,
for though I rightly say I don't agree,
what I do is clearly not enough.
The price we pay for our democracy –
to be invaded by this vile stuff!
Unworthy lies portrayed as honesty –
the price we pay for speech, is far from free.

# When Life is Good

Sparrows crawl through bush's leaves,
while bright orange flowers entice
honeyeaters to come sip on nectar.

Backyard's soundtrack, this warm,
sunny winter afternoon, a combination
of bird tweeting calls and mechanical

grunt of whipper-snipper, hard at work
in the front yard, while overhead
that wide blue sky is once again present.

Silently watching over us, as we all,
humans, birds and others, go about
our day's business, or pleasures.

# Falling

in response to a piece in Gawler Community Gallery

My gaze, captured by perfectly crafted cloud
carrying & distributing a motherload
of rain, to an ocean already brimful of water.
Or is that over land on the horizon, land
where the cloud brings life to plants, and hope
to people in need? The sun, above, & beyond,
that cloud – that brings light, light that bounces
off the waves and highlights motion. Light
bringing the painting to life, with the sun
rising or falling, as the cloud makes stately
progress across the sky, & the rain is falling,
falling, falling, endlessly, & forever more.

# Who Was David Niven Anyway?

If the moon is a balloon,
What are the stars
Shining so brightly? Are they
Promises made & never broken,
Lies untold, taken back, paid for,
& never told again?
Or are the stars reminders
Of possibles, maybes, & perhapses,
Woven tightly together with actuals & reals
So what may be, becomes what is
Eventually – but well before
Those beautiful brightly shining stars
Fade, & then die.

## My Preferred Ways

Quiet contemplation over noisy consternation,
that seems a better way. Wondering, and pondering,
observing much and always learning…
This works well for me.

Watching Nature at its best, flowers, trees, and creatures –
leading me to my finer thoughts and words.
The way birds cooperate, and share their time
when drinking and bathing, birdbath the place to be.

A mix of species, big and small, taking turns,
calmly waiting, each knowing their chance would come.
From multiple small sparrows to larger loner magpies,
with many others in between, the bird bath
is where birds all come to quench their thirst,

while I watch them, from inside unseen,
quenching my own thirst with water too.
Drinking water, and bathing in water too, all of us.
I watch these creatures, think on the sameness,
glad we all live here, sharing many things, together.

## Baby blue

Aussie sky, azure beauty
sun is shining brightly

Happy smiles, summer fun
to warm a winter's frown

Good times on for one and all
booze is sculled down nightly

Drinking games, dangerous
Uncle Joe being a clown

Showing off his lady friend
a queen in her fancy gown

But the stories said about her,
with eager glee they're told,

It seems that gleaming halo
is certainly not made of gold.

# The Big C

The letter is one strong in my life,
my birth name given to me, then
the one I married into. Names
are only words though, no harm
nothing fatal there. But that other
C word, the big one, that's there
in my blood lines, and in my blood?
Mother's breast cancer, quiet now,
but who knows how long the possible
killer may remain in hiding, waiting?
It's a constant reminder that death
is always possible, and inevitably,
eventually, however often you waltz
past, and sidestep it, partnered
by surgeon and other medics, it's
always there… My own forays
into cancer's realms are ongoing
surface issues, not fatal ones, so far,
but they're not surprising, after a life
of too much sun, current medication,
and chemicals. They all add up,
these things, and I wonder will I be
totalled by the Big C, or will it be
something else does the deed?

# The Skin We're In

It wraps us up, snug and tight
It treats us well if we treat it right
Not too cold, not too hot,
Too much sun, you'll get a spot!

And spots can be good or bad
Freckles are cute, cancers are sad
Slice it, and red life leaks out
Band-Aids fix that, without a doubt

Skin is there, from before our birth
It covers us for all our time on Earth
We bash it, bruise it, burn it, accuse it
Treasure it, cherish it, try not to abuse it

Why that spot on my nose that night?
Wanted to look lovely, looked a fright.
Pimpled through my teenage years,
Causing me many anguished tears

I see the marks that wisdom's made
Scars put there by scalpel blade
And other scars where life has been –
The stories shown on skin's big screen.

## Rusty Thoughts

My rusty brain, thoughts
forgotten, ideas fade
away – held only by
fine threads of semi-rational
thought, given to destructive
lines, at times, whimpers,
cries, various kerfuffles,
some idle consternation
and ill thought lies. I shrug,
look around, and see life
continues on, always,
with me, or without me,
constantly, regardless.

# Finding My Starring Role

A primary school failure at netball,
ball skills zero, keenness in game
even lower…horse racing links
through family, led nowhere
really, horses, winners or not
of little interest, despite family.

Many years of motherhood
go sideways, no sports in sight,
until in a brief interlude, when
lawn bowls arrived, & echoes
of other family links reminded me
of quite a different kind of game.

Now, I've played that game, found
and joined my team, learnt rules,
and felt the pride that comes when
bowl meets jack, and stays there,
up close and personal, and you're
playing your part, helping the team –
not a star player, but trying to be
more or less, until came the day,
a challenge given, a decision
to be made. Which would it be,
poetry or lawn bowls? A shocking
question, but poetry easily won…

I'd never realised, this decision
would ever come, and still don't
know why 'both' wasn't an answer
I was allowed to make. But now,
my starring role, is with the poetry,
and watching, not playing bowls.

## Leaving a Mark

Do I, don't I, will I, or won't I?
A tricky choice sometimes to make.
If you get it right, then you're a hero
get it wrong, though, then you're a fake.

See, even those people seem so shiny,
a faker's gold isn't precious, it's just glitter
the metal as fake as the person themselves, if
things get tough, they go, the ultimate quitter…

So if you say you will, but it turns out you can't –
Get in touch, ring up, and tell them, 'I'm sorry, no.'
Honesty is valued, by the people who realise truth,
so when life gets like that, say you can't do it, can't go.

But don't always stay safe, and never try anything new,
it's a cop out that one, in my point of view. If you never try,
that means you can't ever achieve, what kind of life is that?
I want to be remembered for good things I've done, after I die.

# No forgetting some things?

He was the cliché of a rabid wolf
His mouth a dribbling foam of lust
You were too young back then
And so was he, you realise now.

You thought you'd forgotten it all
But some things will slip through
The fog of years, and haunt you
Even in your wiser mature years.

There's no forgetting some things,
you wish you'd known then, all you
know now and you wonder, does he
remember, what you want to forget?

Wisdom earned, lessons learned,
alcohol's awful glamour understood…
Too late now, to change the past
But it's filed under forgive and forget.

# After Bushfires

Tanka

Recent travels
along roads the fires followed
devastation
still to be seen, dead trees
but regeneration too


Thinking of farmers
when growing paddocks, became
killing fields –
stock and native animals
victims of uncaring fire


A gentle breeze now,
I remember other winds –
northerlies, fire stink.
Trees, stock and people all safe,
next time, though, who knows next time?


My Sunday thoughts
about trees and their branches –
how many victims
of fire and damaging winds?
Monday's travels will show me

# Watching

My recent place of recovery
is now just the sofa again,
a sitting spot for us all,
to view sport, drama,
comedy, on TV screen,
with the window, now
my place for seeing life
and love flourishing,
flapping, fluttering,
and feeding. The birds
living their lives,
as I watch…knowing
I can now easily get up
and move around,
no need for extra
assistance. That time
of recovery, showed me
watching and thinking
with nothing to do,
can still bring much,
and am grateful to know it,
as I am grateful too,
that recovery edges
ever closer, to recovered,
and rehabilitation closer
to simply, ordinary life

# It's Just Not Cricket!

after watching some disruptive pigeon antics on TV one summer

I'm watching the cricket, stupid pigeon,
it's got in the way, took a crack to the noggin,
and now carrying on, like it's in the theatre,
putting on a death scene, better than
anything Shakespeare ever wrote!
If the cricketer gets given out over that,
it will be a miscarriage of all the rules
of the game. You may be hurt, pigeon,
but get over it, go to the drinks tent,
and do a bit of 'glamping' – satisfy some
of your humanified so-called instincts.
and get something nice to drink too.
Get off the field, get into some good stuff,
and let the game go one without you!

# Go Team!

We gathered together,
Each of us hoping
To win, but our team,
Our position on the ladder,
Our weaknesses,
Indicated no matter
How well we scrummed,
How ominous we tried
To appear
To our opposition,
It would be
The wooden spoon,
Rather than a gilded
Carousel
Of high-scoring games
That would be
Our inglorious prize
This year
Yet again

# An End of Year Lament

Sitting looking at some lovely trees, appreciating shade and breeze, and contemplating my car situation, with radiator seemingly as f**ked as our nation

Cars that break down, a leader who won't lead,
Neither of them are things I need.
I need a new radiator, one that works,
Nation needs a PM who leads, not shirks.

That radiator, that's easily fixed
Booked in already, that task ticked
But Scomo? Oh please, what can we do?
I reckon he's a dud, d'you think that too?

But how to rid ourselves of this grinning klutz,
With his Coalition of greedy mutts?
I reckon it's time for another election,
One that will lead to a better direction.

Our nation is failing in too many ways
Wisdom forgotten, idiocy stays,
Oh for some real Aussie 'Fair Go',
Do we still remember how to do that, though?

## Deeper Lives

The sky, the horizon, my love for both
Love for people – family, friends
Honesty eternal, it never ends

Truthful engagement, heart and soul –
Follow the sky up to the stars
Or horizon's line that mankind mars

Pathways followed, dead ends, or none
The journey, life's lessons, go where you will
Learning continues if you're breathing still…

Why are we here, do you know? I don't
'Cept failure to learn for what life will give
Makes a lie of a life – you have to LIVE!

Life spent unlived is life spent as a dolt
So many chances, people to love
And opportunities from Nature above

As every pear tree bears better if tended
So a life lived well, will bear fruit too
I love the 'pears' life gives, don't you?

Fossick around, dig deep as you go
Ask questions and listen, open your head,
Don't take easy paths, but good ways instead

Time spent on playthings, wasted on fripperies,
And hours thrown away, on mere lightweight fluff,
These will show you're not thinking enough

Thoughts, ideas, questions and answers
With these you'll get most from your life
Deeper lives come from troubles and strife…

Challenges faced, decisions made and enacted
The tough times show the best possible you
Few of us realise, how much we can do.

## Lest We Forget

And in remembering,
we must never forget
the Hell of War,
as we thank those
who faced that Hell
on our behalf.
May negotiation
and peace, soon become
our default mode,
instead of violence
and destruction

www.ingramcontent.com/pod-product-compliance
Lightning Source LLC
Chambersburg PA
CBHW050308120526
44590CB00016B/2541